D0643879

The Dairy Group

BY KATIE CLARK

Published by The Child's World®
1980 Lookout Drive • Mankato, MN 56003-1705
800-599-READ • www.childsworld.com

Acknowledgments
The Child's World®: Mary Berendes, Publishing Director
Red Line Editorial: Editorial direction
The Design Lab: Design
Amnet: Production
Photographs ©: Front cover: mexrix/Shutterstock Images; FoodIcons; Shutterstock Images; mexrix/Shutterstock Images, 3, 8, 15; Shutterstock Images, 3, 9; Dudarev Mikhail/Shutterstock Images, 4; choosemyplate.gov, 5; FoodIcons, 6, 8; BrandX Images, 7, 11; Somchai Som/Shutterstock Images, 10; Kids in Motion, 13; Sergey Nivens/Shutterstock Images, 14; Thomas_EyeDesign/iStockPhoto, 16; El Nariz/Shutterstock Images, 17, 23; ComStock, 18; Morgan Lane Photography/Shutterstock Images, 19; margouillat photo/Shutterstock Images, 21

ISBN: 978-1623236021
LCCN: 2013931362

Printed in the United States of America
Mankato, MN
July, 2013
PA02178

ABOUT THE AUTHOR

Katie Clark has been making up stories since she was a little girl. Now that she's grown she spends her time reading, writing, and playing make-believe with her daughters. Katie's writing for children has appeared in numerous publications, including books and magazines.

Table of Contents

CHAPTER ONE

What Is Dairy?

Have you ever seen a dairy farm? Maybe you see rolling hills dotted with cows. Perhaps the barns are filled with large, loud machines. The machines might be hooked to large jugs filled with milk. Getting the milk and making dairy foods are not easy. Living on a farm keeps you busy. You have to feed the animals, milk the cows, and keep the animals healthy. So what good is all of that work? What is the big deal about dairy?

Milk is used in many ways. Many people pour it over their breakfast cereal. Some people drink milk, and others use it for cooking or baking. You can use milk to make other foods, too. Yogurt, cheese, and butter are all made with milk.

▼ **Cows provide the milk used to make dairy foods.**

▶ **Opposite page: Use the MyPlate diagram to make healthy eating choices.**

Fruits
Grains
Dairy
Vegetables
Protein
ChooseMyPlate.gov

Milk is a dairy food. Dairy is one of the main food groups on MyPlate. It is one of the building blocks of a healthy diet. Dairy provides **nutrients** we all need to be healthy. The MyPlate guidelines show us how to eat to grow strong and healthy. Kids ages four to eight should eat or drink 2 1/2 cups of dairy every day. Kids between nine and 13 years old need 3 cups of dairy every day.

Milk is not the only popular dairy food. Yogurt and cheese are also favorites. Yogurt is full of **minerals** such as

◀ **It's important to drink or eat 2 1/2 to 3 cups of dairy foods every day.**

▶ **Opposite page: Milk is a healthy drink that goes with breakfast, lunch, or dinner.**

calcium and potassium. These help keep the body healthy. Yogurt is a food made from milk. To make yogurt, the milk is heated. When the milk is hot, **bacteria** are added to turn the sugars in the milk to acid. This makes the milk thicken and gives it a tangy flavor. Now it is yogurt! Flavors can be added when the yogurt is set. Vanilla and fruit flavors such as strawberry and blueberry are popular, but plain yogurt is good, too.

Another food that comes from milk is cheese. Cheese is full of **protein**. Protein gives you strong muscles. It takes 10 pounds of milk to make 1 pound of cheese. The milk is poured into a giant

▲ **Yogurt is a tangy treat for breakfast or a snack.**

▲ **Cheese is a dairy food that is packed with protein.**

HARDWORKING DAIRY COWS

Every year, over nine million cows are milked in America. One cow can make up to four hundred glasses of milk a day! Farmers use machines to extract the milk from cows on a dairy farm. After the cows are milked, the milk is pasteurized. This means it is boiled to kill bad bacteria. Did you know that dairy cows are not the only animals used for their milk? Other milking animals include goats, sheep, buffalo, camels, and reindeer.

tub. It is heated and boiled until it begins to get chunky. It is stirred as it thickens. Then it is left to harden. Once the cheese is hard, all of the extra milk and water is drained away. Now the cheese can be cut into wheels or blocks for cutting and shredding.

Milk, yogurt, and cheese are three of the most popular dairy products. Others include dessert foods such as pudding and ice cream. Although some foods are made from milk, they lose too much calcium during the cooking process. These foods are not considered dairy products anymore. Cream cheese and butter are two foods made from milk that have no calcium.

CHAPTER TWO

How Is Dairy Good for You?

Dairy is good for the body. MyPlate says kids ages four to 13 need 2 1/2 to 3 cups of dairy every day. Why is dairy so good for us? It is full of the **vitamins** and minerals kids need.

Dairy is full of calcium. Calcium is a mineral that makes strong bones. When bones are weak, they can break. That hurts! Calcium also helps your blood **clot** when you get bruises or scrapes. This means it helps your body stop bleeding. It also makes your heart strong. Eat and drink lots of

▲ Milk contains calcium that helps your bones grow strong.

▶ Opposite page: The calcium and potassium in dairy foods keep your bones and heart strong so you can play sports.

calcium if you want strong bones and healthy blood.

Another mineral found in dairy foods is potassium. The heart pumps blood and oxygen through the body. Potassium makes the heart strong so it can keep pumping. A kid with a weak heart would get tired easily. It would be hard to breathe and think. It would be difficult to run and play.

Vitamin D is a vitamin often added to dairy foods. It helps the body absorb calcium. This means it helps the body soak up calcium like a sponge. Vitamin D can also help keep bones strong and skin healthy. Eating foods **fortified** with vitamin D can help you get enough of the nutrient. You can also get vitamin D by soaking up sunlight.

VITAMIN D

The body needs vitamin D. Vitamin D can be found in foods, but it can also be found in sunshine. Sunshine is the most natural form of vitamin D. Spending 15 minutes a day in the sun can give you the vitamin D you need every day. Make sure you use sunscreen if you stay in the sun for longer than 15 minutes. Sunscreen will protect you from the sun's harmful rays.

Protein is found in dairy, too. It helps keep the muscles strong. Kids need strong muscles for lots of things. Strong muscles help you run, jump, and climb. They give kids the power to stay active. Eating dairy will help your body get what it needs to stay healthy.

▸ **Power up on the protein in dairy foods!**

▲ **A cup of yogurt counts as one serving of dairy.**

◀ **Opposite page: Milk helps your body recharge after playing outside.**

CHAPTER THREE

How Much Dairy Do You Need?

The MyPlate guide is split into five basic food groups: fruits, vegetables, dairy, grains, and protein. The guidelines tell you how much of each type of food you need.

Dairy is one of the building blocks of a healthy diet and part of the MyPlate guidelines. Low-fat or fat-free dairy foods will give you the nutrients you need without adding too many **calories** to your diet. MyPlate shows that kids ages four to eight need 2 1/2 cups of dairy every day. Kids between

CALORIES
Calories are tiny bits of energy. They give us strength to run and play. Not eating enough calories can be bad for us. We would not have enough energy to move or think. Eating too many calories can be bad for us, too. This would make our bodies unhealthy and gain weight. It is important to eat the right amount of calories so we can stay active and be healthy.

◀ Opposite page: Pour skim or soy milk over your breakfast cereal.

nine and 13 years old need 3 cups of dairy each day. A glass of milk, two slices of cheddar cheese, and an 8-ounce cup of yogurt all count as 1 cup of dairy. Other foods made with milk also count as dairy foods, such as frozen yogurt. You can use calcium-fortified soy milk to meet your dairy needs, too.

Getting enough dairy is easy. You can drink a glass of skim milk for breakfast. Skim milk is milk

▶ Top your chili with cheddar cheese for a creamy twist on a cold-weather meal.

that has had its fat removed. Or you could pour skim milk or soy milk over your breakfast cereal. Some people like to start their day with a cup of fat-free yogurt mixed with a handful of granola.

Lunch is also a great time to eat dairy foods. Eat a fat-free cheese stick or a cup of yogurt with your lunch at school. Wash your lunch down with a glass of cold skim milk. Eating dairy with dinner is easy. Sprinkle some shredded cheddar cheese over your chili or some Parmesan cheese on your spaghetti. Gulp down another glass of skim milk. For a treat, eat a scoop of vanilla pudding or fruity frozen yogurt for dessert.

Now you know how important dairy can be. Without dairy you would not have a strong body. This is why MyPlate tells you to eat lots of it!

▲ **Dairy foods keep your body strong and growing.**

▶ **Try each of these dairy foods to eat the MyPlate way!**

Hands-on Activity: Create Your Own Yogurt Flavor

Wouldn't it be fun to create your own yogurt flavor?

What You'll Need:

Cup of plain yogurt, fruit

Directions:

1. First, start with a cup of plain yogurt.
2. Then, add your favorite fruit or fruit flavors.
3. Stir well and enjoy!

Can you think of any yummy yogurt combinations? Here are a few ideas: blueberries and lemon juice, strawberries and bananas, blueberries and granola. Adding fruits, granola, and nuts will help you eat from four of the food groups—fruits, grains, protein, and dairy!

Glossary

bacteria (bak-TEER-ee-ul): Bacteria are organisms so small you cannot see them. Though some bacteria cause illness, most will not harm you and many are good for you.

calcium (KAL-see-um): Calcium is an essential nutrient. Calcium helps build strong bones and teeth.

calories (KAL-ur-eez): Calories are measurements of energy found in food. Kids need calories to play sports and do well in school.

clot (klot): To clot is to stick together. Calcium helps blood clot.

extract (eks-TRAKT): To extract is to take out. Dairy farm machines extract milk from cows.

fortified (FORT-i-fiyd): Fortified means something was made strong by adding more of a certain ingredient. Milk is often fortified with vitamin D.

minerals (MIN-er-ulz): Minerals are substances found in foods. Minerals help the body stay healthy.

nutrients (NOO-tree-entz): Nutrients are substances the body needs to grow. Vitamins and minerals are nutrients.

pasteurized (PAS-chur-izd): When something is pasteurized, it is exposed to high temperatures to kill bad germs. Drink pasteurized milk to avoid harmful bacteria.

protein (PRO-teen): Protein is a part of food that provides energy and contains building blocks used by the whole body. Protein is found in meat, nuts, and seeds.

vitamins (VYE-tuh-minz): Vitamins are substances found in foods that help the body stay healthy. Vitamins are found in fruits and vegetables.

To Learn More

BOOKS

Graimes, Nicola. *Kids' Fun and Healthy Cookbook*. New York: DK Press, 2007.

Owen, Ruth. *Milk! Life on a Dairy Farm*. New York: Windmill Books, 2012.

WEB SITES

Visit our Web site for links about dairy: **childsworld.com/links**

Note to Parents, Teachers, and Librarians: We routinely verify our Web links to make sure they are safe and active sites. So encourage your readers to check them out!

Index